# CAT SENSE

*A Feline Style for Living*

KAREN FARRELL

MANSARD BOOKS
NEW YORK

ISBN-10: 0615523684

ISBN-13: 9780615523682

www.mansardbooks.com

For Terrence

*Making friends with a cat*
*can only be a profitable experience.*

COLETTE

# *Introduction*

✕ ✕ ✕

**THE NOTION THAT** darling domesticated cats are kissin' kin to such an extinct subspecies of felines as the Saber Toothed Cat can be alarming, but therein lies much of their charm. Be they tigers or Tonkinese, pumas or Persians, cats are courageous, languid, and curious. They can also have hissy fits and snub anyone who has offended them. In short, they are much like people, though perhaps cuter and sometimes fluffier. What you can gain from the cat is not dissimilar to what is found in any journey of discovery. After longingly searching for enlightenment, the seeker invariably comes to realize that the source of illumination shines from within. Humans often cannot readily see their true interior longings or, indeed, notice opportunities that exist all around. Cats, though, see much and can show the way to enjoying life more fully. This book is an adventure in rediscovering yourself. It is the cat's retelling of something you may have forgotten–how to navigate in the world with style and grace. As memory is sometimes woefully short, this is a book that can serve as a reminder, one that can be picked up and referenced often. It is a collection that can help you retrieve what has never truly been lost. Like all of those feline friends, you can learn to tread lightly through life and take pleasure in the trip. So make like a cat and curl up in a warm, comfy spot. Open this treasure hunt of a book, with the cat as tour guide, and find the gems for living that await you inside.

# *Act naturally*

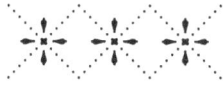

✦ ✦ ✦

**THE MANX CAT,** which is said to have originated in the Isle of Man, is virtually tailless. As the result of having longer back legs than front ones, some Manx cats even have a hopping gait, like a rabbit. Is it a cabbit? No, it's a cat through and through. In addition to the elongated hind quarters and truncated tail, Manx cats that hop may also have a spinal deformity. Whatever the origin of these physical anomalies, the Manx is not phased by its exceptional nature. This feline just goes about the business of being a cat. Whatever handicaps you may have, carry on. Like the Manx, act naturally!

# Aim high

* * *

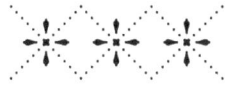

CATS HAVE THE ability to jump seven times their height. They have been known to jump fences that may even be considerably taller. If you are going to aim high, why not target your personal best. Shoot for the topmost goal that you can imagine. Once there, you may be capable of reaching even greater heights. The object is not so much attaining those lofty bull's-eyes as it is the thrill of the pursuit and the energy that you put into action.

# Assume a calm demeanor

* * *

CATS OFTEN SEEM to be impervious to their surroundings. Their nature appears to be unflappable. No wonder so many people adore having them around. Cats lend a calming influence. You can try fostering their serene nature. Imagine yourself quietly and unperturbedly taking stock of the world around you. Notice times when you find yourself becoming unduly anxious. Remind yourself to take several deep breaths and relax into them. Reset your gauge on how you measure any given situation. You may just find that, as a result, you conduct yourself in a more composed manner, one fashioned after the cat!

*Banish the words*
*"I have nothing to wear"*

✳ ✳ ✳

**SIMPLE BLACK TIE** elegance is the hallmark of the cat. No obsessing about wardrobes. Cats have a signature birthday uniform and they stick with it. They act as though this scheme is thoroughly fine and so it is. Although a single glittering diamond necklace would nicely set off many a jeweled cat eye, they take to the unadorned, understated look. Felines shed hair like they are tossing off a "so last season's" coat. They teach us all that the right cattitude makes one's beauty unassailable.

# Be a noble soul

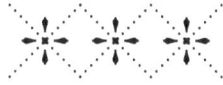

✳ ✳ ✳

**REMEMBER THE FABLE** of the lion plagued by a splinter lodged in one of its paws?  In one version, a courageous little mouse comes along and removes the painful sliver.  The lion, not forgetting this kind act, later rescues the mouse from danger. Story also has it that when Edgar Allen Poe's wife was deathly ill, the writer's cat stayed in bed with the frail woman until she breathed her last breath.  Centuries-old legend  tells of cats visiting their masters imprisoned in The Tower of London.  One prisoner, poorly fed, was grateful when his cat hunted birds and brought them as gifts to him.  His jailer cooked up the fowl, providing the cat's owner with his only nutritious meals.  In recent times, cats have been known to travel long distances, without the aid of GPS, to reunite with their adopted families. Be as steadfast as the loyal cat and you join the ranks of those with true nobility.

# Be a practiced party animal

✳ ✳ ✳

**EVEN AMIDST THE** social swirl, cats know when to quit the party. Finding a lull in any festivity, cats know that it's time to "high-tail-it" out of there. They won't stick around to drink the leftover wine, nor should you. It would be most unbecoming. They don't chase after the unsustainable high. Having surfeited on life's feast, they contentedly take their leave. Even if you discover that you are the life of the party, still make your own dignified, and timely, exit.

# Be a reassuring presence

✳ ✳ ✳

**REMEMBER THE OLD** saying about someone really being able to "get your goat" when you feel perturbed? This adage harkens back to the belief that the way to quiet down an upset horse was to, well, "get your goat". In racing circles, trainers have been known to get cats, instead of goats, to sooth their thoroughbred horses. These stable companions have provided equanimity to many a troubled mount. The presence of feline friends has eased horses into peaceful slumber, preparing high-strung colts and fillies for peak performance at high stakes races. You can use this racing tip by remembering others in distress. Like the cat with the racehorse, you can be a calming influence by making time to be with a friend in crisis or by visiting some-one sick in the hospital. No doubt you will both feel better for it. Borrowing from racing parlance, together you will win the "Daily Double".

# *Be a rebel with your own cause*

✦✦✦

**UNABASHEDLY LOOKING OUT** for its own aims is the cause of the cat. It is no poster child, that is, poster kitten, for the unactualized. A cat knows what it wants and is adroit at getting it. Although you may not be slaying dragons, follow the cat's lead and you can be true to your authentic self. While others may waver, hold steady to your convictions. Give yourself permission to be a rebel with your own cause—a cause detailing your most passionate dreams.

# Be a social animal

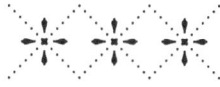

*‡‑ ‡‑ ‡*

LIONS ARE KNOWN to group together in prides. By so doing, they gain strength in numbers. When they hunt together, as they often do, they are able to bring down prey much larger then themselves. Although the lion is universally referred to as the King of Beasts, it is the camaraderie and teamwork of the pride that assure the success of their hunt and their continued survival. Social life has many mutual benefits essential for humanity's survival as well. Cooperation builds communities and nations. On a personal level, social life can strengthen your spirit and renew a sense of stewardship.

# *Be a thespian*

✳ ✳ ✳

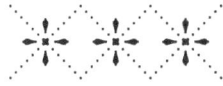

**ONE MINUTE A** cat may be slinking across the room in film-noir fashion and the next instant gazing guilelessly into your eyes. It can gracefully wave its tail while lounging and then poise that same tail to balance some tightrope act across a narrow mantle. Cats suit the behavior to the occasion. How refreshing to see this candid comportment. Follow their lead. By being less self-conscious and able to stay in the moment, you will play your part well on the stage of life.

# *Be compassionate*

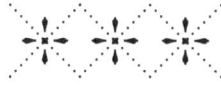

✢ ✢ ✢

HAVE YOU EVER noticed the sensitivity that a cat may have towards you when you are feeling sad? Cats rate very high on the scale of social intelligence. The breed of Russian Blues, in particular, is generally anything but blue. They are known for being cheerful and perceptive to the moods in their environment. Typically, they will sense a household member who is feeling gloomy and, as a way of offering comfort, perhaps extend a soothing paw.

In this sometimes heartaching world, you can lend kind words of support to someone greatly in need of solace. By reaching out, you could make all the difference.

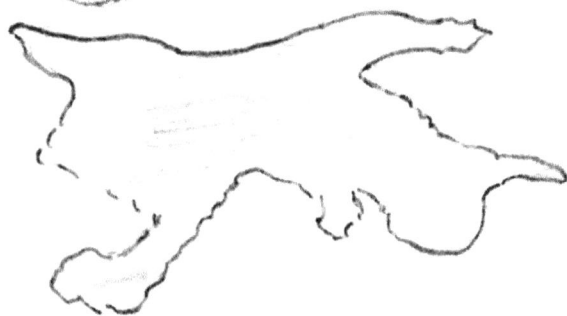

# *Be full of whimsy*

✳ ✳ ✳

**THE CAPRICIOUS NATURE** of cats is one of the traits that fascinates and charms. Their silliness and high jinx are endearing qualities. Watching them allows us to vicariously enter their childlike kingdom. Their playfulness invites us in and gives us license to be fanciful too. You can adopt this whimsical nature by being madcap, game for amusement, and able to revel in the ridiculous, the impractical and yet, paradoxically, the sublime.

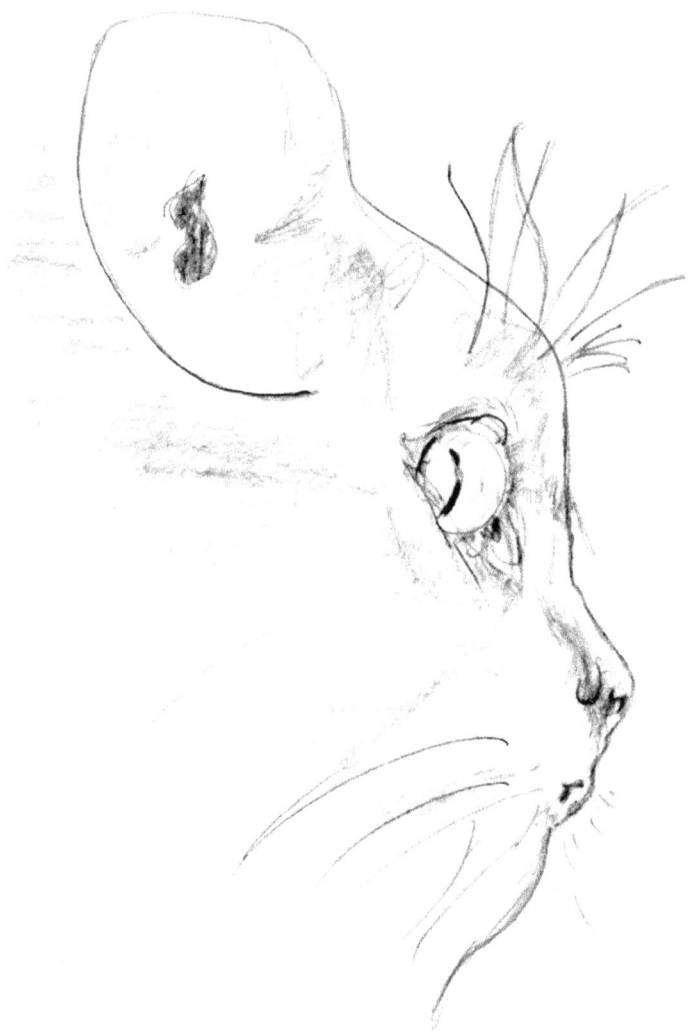

*Be prepared*

✳ ✳ ✳

**WHISKERS LOCATED ON** both a cat's face and legs act as an additional sensory device when lighting is low. Embedded three times deeper and with twice the thickness of other hairs, whiskers, called vibrissae, act as subtle detectors of air currents, aiding cats in determining size, shape and location of objects in the dark. Next time you are venturing outside at night, take a flashlight with you, first checking that the batteries are in good working order. When a storm kicks up or other factors cause power outages, operating in the dark can be quite disorienting. At home, have safely enclosed candles and a lighter or matches at the ready. While inside, you might also want to carefully try testing your ability to move about in the dark. Studies show that this type of orienting helps your brain to develop more of its own neural pathways!

# Begin to soar

*❋ ❋ ❋*

SNOW LEOPARDS ARE magnificent leapers.  Equipped with short front legs and long, powerful hindquarters, they are well suited to the rugged and mountainous terrain in which they live.  They can jump a distance of nearly 50 feet.  These big cats needn't have all of the fun.  You can dream of flying through the air like these tremendous felines or, if you can, bound outside like the house cat does and enjoy your own exhilarating version of soaring, be it rock hopping, puddle jumping or leapfrogging!

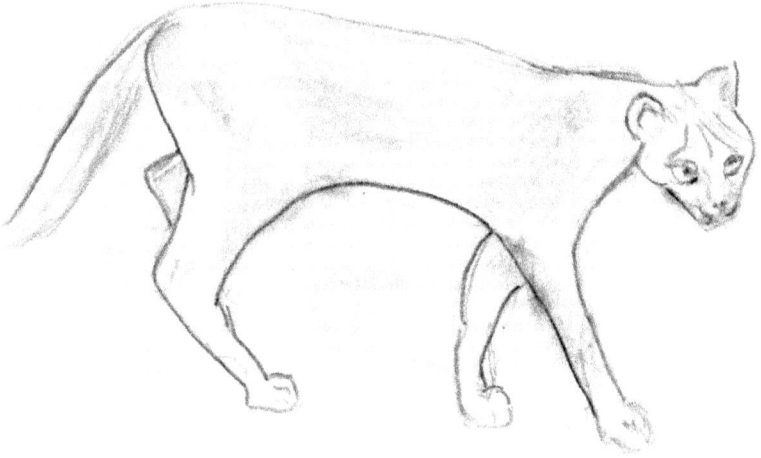

# *Broaden your repertoire*

✳ ✳ ✳

**WEASEL-LIKE EARS,** long neck, slender body and a pointy head make for one of the most unusual looking of the small cats–the Jaguarundi. It is also one of the most adaptable. The Jaguarundi lives amidst thorny brush and other impenetrable areas as a safeguard against predators. Where available, they set up housekeeping close to water, thereby assuring a ready supply of fish. Able to whistle, chatter, and chirp like a bird, Jaguarundi have an undoubtedly useful repertoire of sound effects. Even with short legs, these cats move about quickly, employing an effective darting technique in pursuit of their prey. Versatility in the practical arts of hunting, swimming, fishing and birding over a large territory makes for a Renaissance cat. Revitalize your own interests and gain mastery of new things. As a result, you too can enjoy the fruits of your varied accomplishments.

# Carve out some privacy

＊ ＊ ＊

CATS KEEP A low profile when they want a break. They find all sorts of ways to escape. Cats know that they can relax more when they are unobserved, out of one's mind and one's sight. They acknowledge what busy humans sometimes ignore. While public space is a necessary element in any society, private space is a bastion from that same society. Remember that you need a bit of seclusion to refresh the spirit!

# *Catch up on sleep*

✳ ✳ ✳

**CATS DOZE SOMEWHERE** in the vicinity of sixteen hours out of every twenty-four—getting twice as much sleep, on average, as humans. Because they are so well rested, they are game for action when they wake up. Many people need at least eight, if not nine or ten hours of sleep each night to feel fully rested. Make a hefty deposit in your sleep account and reap big dividends in terms of your energy and alertness. If you missed a few winks, try an afternoon cat nap. By getting needed rest, you'll be equal to the challenges of the day.

# Check it out first

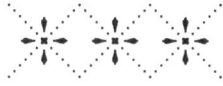

* * *

CATS DO NOT charge into new associations with others. They take things slowly. They sniff around. When houseguests come, for example, cats smell the shoes and check out the luggage. They might remain aloof or make themselves scarce until which time they feel that the visitors warrant getting to know a little better. When meeting someone new or when contemplating a new business agreement, for example, you may find that a good dose of caution gives you additional time to be more discerning. You can remain open to possibilities and still keep your antennae up. Before entering into any new alliance, by checking it out first, you allow others to earn your trust.

# Climb to the top

✳ ✳ ✳

**WHILE NOT ALTOGETHER** arboreal, many cats like to climb trees, posts, curtains, nearly anything in sight. One Swiss feline is even known to have quietly followed a group of mountaineers climbing to the top of the Matterhorn. Having much shorter legs, the stalwart cat still made it to the summit. Climbing may be one of the cat's secrets to having such a svelte body.

You likewise can obtain a beautiful silhouette by doing things like climbing the stairs instead of taking the elevator. You not only get exercise but save electricity! Exercise also powers up those feel-good endorphins. Keep climbing those heights and, before long, you'll be in top shape to enjoy the view.

# Communicate succinctly

CATS RESERVE A *mot juste* meant only for humans – the meow. This plaintive vocalization is not used to converse with other cats. Since this spare and elegant sound is reserved exclusively for human ears, it carries more meaning. One simple meow really gets to the point.

Remembering to be brief in your remarks makes you more effective. As well, brevity provides welcome relief to the often information-overloaded listener. Sometimes the repetition of a central word or idea is better than a lot of excess chatter. Meow... meow.

# Concentrate like a cat

✳ ✳ ✳

**HAVE YOU EVER** seen a cat fully engaged in the act of chasing a moving object or exploring newfound nooks and crannies? It is absorbed in a tide of delight. Time appears to be suspended as the cat is swept up in the deep concentration of the moment. You can model the cat's engrossed state by delving into a pursuit that you enjoy immensely. In the process, you may well experience flow–that highly sought-after state of immersion that transcends time.

# Consider other dimensions

CATS RESTORE FAITH in the unseen. Because of their unique structure, cats' eyes absorb more light, enabling them to see with six times the sensitivity of humans. With such keen sight, cats can perceive things humans cannot discern. Their vision provides a glimpse into the unknown. They love to play with phantoms of their own devising. Who knows? Maybe they actually see ghosts that lie out there beyond human perception. How marvelous it is to imagine that alternate realities do exist, beyond the visible world as we know it. Cats serve as a reminder that this may well be so. You may find that believing in other dimensions makes your life more magical!

# Cultivate the patience of a cat

✛ ✛ ✛

**CATS CAN WAIT** for seemingly interminable periods of time for the chance to hunt one of their favorites, be it a mouse, a bird or a fish. In this era of immediate gratification, it is a refreshing departure to actually exercise patience. The rewards can be great. Assume a certain cat-like anticipation as you await your opportunity. The trick is timing. Once you get your chance, recognize it and act on it. Like the cat exercising patience in pursuit of the prize, once gained, it will taste all the sweeter.

# Digest a lot of material

✴ ✴ ✴

**THE TIGER IS** not only the biggest member of the cat family but it is also the largest stalking hunter on earth. A tiger can pack away a 65 pound meal. This is not to suggest that you become a glutton. Considering food metaphorically, as in "food for thought", you can consume volumes of books and be fortified with knowledge. Instead of the cat's 65 pounds of meat, try reading 65 pages a day of a meaty non-fiction work, a how-to book or a literary novel that has stood the test of time. Like the huge meal that the tiger digests, you will absorb material that will enrich your life and, as with the tiger, you will be better nourished for life's journey.

# Discover what's "in the air"

✳ ✳ ✳

**IN ADDITION TO** a normal sense of smell, cats, like some other species, have an extra sensitivity to smell known as the Flehmen's response. It is triggered by an organ located in the cat's mouth, behind the front teeth. Called the Jacobson's organ – it connects to the nasal cavity and provides additional information regarding a scent. By slightly opening the mouth and curling the upper lip, the cat draws smells into this organ. This "flehmening" process enables cats to gain news about a food source, for example, or detect the location of a potential mate. You too can take time to investigate your surroundings. In so doing, you might discover a new eatery, a great place to socialize or a terrific parking spot. Be nosy! Sniff around to get a hint of what's "in the air."

# Do more with yarn than knit your brow

TAKING UP A relaxing hobby, like knitting or crocheting, is to model one's life after a cat. You both can have fun with a ball of yarn. Knitting is also highly portable and versatile. It can be done as a social activity or while lounging at home in a favorite easy chair. You can sandwich knitting into your lunch breaks, while standing in line at the post office, or to soothe yourself while waiting for test results. Using your hands to make something tangible can be not only rewarding but practical as well. You may discover that taking up knitting, or any other form of needlecraft, can be a great way to unwind!

# Do the legwork

*⁘ ⁘ ⁘*

**CATS NEED TO** do a lot of walking in their hunt for food in the wild. Strong legs are essential for the pursuit of lunch. Cats need to stay in shape. Once they spot a potential meal, they require those well-toned muscles to prime them for the chase.

Exercising your leg muscles by walking can strengthen you to pursue your dreams. Both literally and figuratively, doing the legwork helps you to achieve any goal that you target. For felines are the first to show you that it's a rat race out there!

# Do you have too much on your plate?

✦✦✦

**CATS LITERALLY GET** turned off when they see too much food in their dinner bowl. They only want to eat the size equivalent of, let's say, a little mouse or a small bird. Anything more than that is distasteful to feline sensibilities. A cat may shy away from food being presented in such an unappetizing way. Do you have too much on your plate, not only at mealtime but in life? You can focus more fully when you have less to process. Lighten up. Having more frequent and smaller meals may be helpful in providing you with greater energy. Dividing your to-do list into bite-sized portions may help you to manage your time better. As a result, you may be surprised at how good you become at cleaning your plate—and your schedule!

*Do you need to stand on ceremony?*

✴✴✴

**THEY MAY STAND** on your important papers. They may stand on your tables, your countertops, your favorite sweater, but cats will generally not stand on ceremony. They are actually downright informal at times, peaceful and unassuming. When you get the urge to insist that everything be done to perfection, just think of that carefree cat, and relax that stickler in you!

# Dress for the cold

✳ ✳ ✳

**HIGH IN THE** Himalayas, on rocky terrain above the timber line, dwells the Snow Leopard. They live in remote regions that would be uninhabitable for any other cat. While they have a durable, stocky frame, they are aided by having a deep, thick coat of fur as protection from the bitter cold. The tail of the Snow Leopard, nearly as long as its body and thick with stores of fat, is flexible enough to wrap around to shield its face when sleeping, much like a cozy muff.

Generally, wild cats have two layers of fur, an overcoat as well as a good lining! A soft, fine undercoat is covered with coarser and longer hair. In cold weather, you can model their dress code. Wearing multiple layers, hats and scarves also help you enjoy even glacial winter cold. Mittens anyone?

# Engage in the present

✦✦✦

**ONE OF THE** principle charms of cats is their ability to engage in the moment. They ground us in the here and now. With timeless composure, they demonstrate that this instant is "the all" of life. You too can certainly embrace the mystery of this temporal realm. Without a rueful backward glance to the past or an anxious look to the future, enjoy the ever-ephemeral present.

# Enjoy the nightlife

✳ ✳ ✳

CATS TEND TO be not only nocturnal but also fond of twilight. Although cats hunt after dark, their prowling can begin at dusk, when the dim light seems just right. By high noon, cats are generally settling in for a siesta. As Noel Coward once sang "Only mad dogs and Englishmen go out in the midday sun." Certainly kitty cats do not sally forth in the blazing light and heat of the day if they can help it. They get their best work done after dark. "Burning the midnight oil" inside, when all is quiet, may help you to get more accomplished. You might find that stepping out at night can also be fun. Figure out your own daily rhythms and you could find yourself enjoying some beautiful nocturnes!

# Enjoy your vocation

✳ ✳ ✳

CATS THROUGHOUT THE ages have focused on one thing—hunting. Being the most spectacular carnivores, they have enjoyed the job. They love a warm meal and are eager to chase after it. Because of this obvious interest and talent, cats have been given positions as "mousers" in any number of settings. Starting in the granaries of the Middle East at the dawn of civilization, cats have been eliminating vermin ever since. Today they can be found prowling the beat in libraries, museums, post offices, hotels and distilleries as resident rodent catchers the world over. Capable and devoted workers, they have been quite able to earn their keep. The record number of mice caught by a single cat exceeds 28,000. Now that's a body of work! Model the cat by generating a life's mission of your own. Be it carpentry or care giving, begin creating your opus now!

# Explore

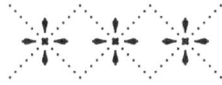

IT HAS BEEN theorized that carnivores, big cats among them, have needed to range about larger territories due to the relative rarity of meat versus grasses and vegetation. Think only of the food chain to recognize that it gets more difficult the higher up you go. Cats are obligate carnivores. Their diet consists almost exclusively of meat. Although some cats do eat plant matter, generally it is only used as an emetic. Unlike fixed vegetation, the cats' prey move about, becoming elusive targets. Cat territories reflect this fact as sometimes they need to push their boundaries further out in search of food. If you cover a lot of ground, you too may well reap a bounty of opportunities. You can explore by beginning to move outside of your comfort zone. What you find beyond the border might well sustain you.

# Extract the most out of life

✛ ✛ ✛

WEIGHING ONLY 5 lbs., the variously named Sand Cat, Dune Cat or Sand-Dune cat is a wild feline of the Sahara desert region. Its diet consists of jerboas, which hop, and other desert rodents, reptiles and large insects. Because of the arid climate and resultant scarcity of water, the sand cat can live solely on the body fluids that it extracts from eating its prey. Talk about getting the most out of life. Tawny coloration is great camouflage for this dune cat and hairy feet enable it to walk on the hot desert sand. You can learn thrift and adaptability from these survivors. They demonstrate how to adjust to the environment by blending in, by taking precautions when out in the elements and by maximizing the use of available resources.

# Find your way out of a paper bag

❈ ❈ ❈

**CAN'T FIND YOUR** way out of a paper bag? Just watch a cat in action when it gets itself virtually wrapped up in a brown sack. Does it want to get out? Who knows? It's enjoying itself with a very unfussy toy. In an age of sophistication and complexity, sometimes simple toys are the best. Cats playing with paper bags are a reminder of this fact. Take the raw materials of this common brown sack. You could fold elaborate origami figures out of it and even learn a little about geometry in the process. You could cut out silhouettes or wall designs. You get the picture. Sometimes simplicity is the building block, the road map for exploring the world. As the cat shows, amusing yourself with a paper bag may lead to a "way out trip"!

# *Follow the money*

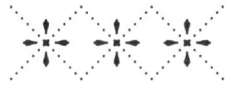

✦ ✦ ✦

**LIONS ARE KNOWN** to have power in numbers when it comes to overtaking "big game". This strategy only fails to work if food sources are in short supply. For that situation, lions will change their tactic and disperse. They know that it is better for the pride to split up and spread out when there are slim pickings in the meal plan. If there is a scarcity of work in one market, you may want to consider moving to an area that has a thriving economy. Like the big cats, going where there are better prospects, you help ensure that you are able to "bring home the bacon." The move needn't be geographical. Find a niche market and you too may find yourself making milLIONS!

# *Follow up*

✳ ✳ ✳

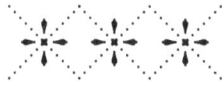

**CATS ARE GOOD** at marking their territory; they are also good at returning to it. Making the rounds of their own already-sprayed boundary is routine. They check for any intervening activity. Maybe other animals have come along to sign the guestbook with their own particular signature spray. Cats may have to reinforce their perimeter markings by respraying certain areas. Maintaining their territory is good follow up work for them. Cats do it as a matter of course. You can follow the lead of the cat. It is a common belief that it generally takes three weeks to ensure that a new habit sticks. Make it a practice to routinely follow up on your leads, hunches and ideas. Persevering in this good habit will help to make all of your endeavors successful ones.

# Gaze to amaze

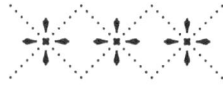

**CATS OFTEN LOOK** intently into people's eyes. They give their undivided attention as they gaze. In many cultures, this is quite polite and flattering. You too can honor the people with whom you are engaging by giving your complete attention to them and by intently listening to what they have to say. Making eye contact and showing interest in others, without distraction, is not only good manners but is also a great validation of our fellow travelers in this life.

# Get caught in the headlights

✳ ✳ ✳

**CATS HAVE THOSE** amazing eyes that glow in the dark when a beam of light shines on them. Compliments of the "tapetum lucidum" (Latin for bright tapestry), this phenomenon is present in a variety of nocturnal animals. The super-abundance of mirroring cells that help cats to see in the dark enables their eyes to reflect any available light. Likewise, this ability has applications for human survival too. Wear reflective gear. Add mirrors and reflectors to your bikes and cars for night time rides so that other vehicles can see you. Put safety first and live to see another day!

# *Get the big picture*

✳ ✳ ✳

**CATS HAVE IT** over humans as far as seeing the big picture. They have greater binocular vision and a larger visual field. In the 70 degrees where they can't automatically see, they rotate their heads to get a more precise view. Cats need this ability to assure their accuracy when hunting. Many people sit at their computers or work tables and forget to look up and gaze out in the distance to relax their eyes and extend their sights. Getting so wrapped up in daily routines can also limit your ability to see beyond the customary view. Life passes you by when you forget to take time, both literally and figuratively, to see "the big picture." Like the cat, expand your perspective and become a person of vision.

# Give off good
## vibrations

✳ ✳ ✳

THE PURR IS a tonal buzz sound made by cats. Speculation as to the nature of this communication varies, anything from signaling their emotional state to expressing goodwill. It is popularly conjectured that cats purr as a self-soothing mechanism, not only when they are blissfully happy but also when they are in pain. If the purr acts as a way to calm them, what a nice internal massage they are able to self-administer. Sighing in humans achieves the same soothing effect. The cat's purr demonstrates a wonderful way to smooth out the jagged edges of life. Sighing can be adopted as your own version of the purr. Remember, when you are trying to gear down from a distressing scenario, to let out a big sigh of relief. Now that's sending out some good vibrations!

# *Go digital!*

✳ ✳ ✳

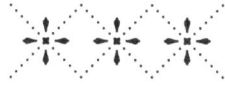

CATS HAVE A great capacity to stay on top of things in their environment. One of the reasons they move quickly is that they belong to the group known as digitigrades. That is, they walk on their toes, or digits! By being alert–and literally on their toes–cats are better able to track down dinner. Go digital and see how much you can accomplish. Staying "on your toes" keeps you sharp and makes you aware of opportunities around you.

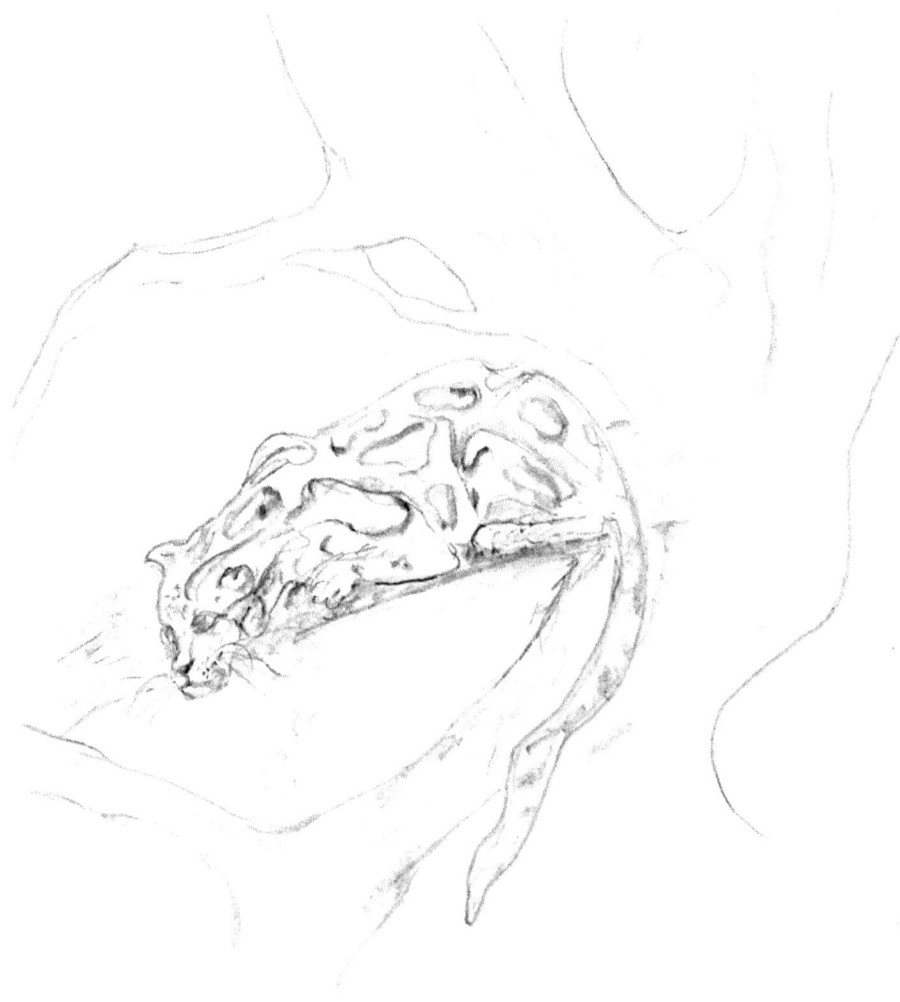

# *Go incognito*

✳ ✳ ✳

CATS LOVE TO go in disguise. Take the clouded leopard as an example. At a young age cubs begin to develop markings and coloring that will serve to camouflage them throughout their lives. Sometimes it's fun to quietly mix in with the scenery. Being able to blend into a crowd can not only keep the fans and paparazzi at bay, but also an exceedingly inquisitive neighbor. The cover can keep you feeling relaxed and part of the flow of humanity. Cats have the right idea—keep a low profile. This way, you can easily slip in, unnoticed. So don those sunglasses, wide-brimmed hat and nondescript clothing and make your anonymous appearance!

# Go "where Angoras fear to tread"?

✳ ✳ ✳

**WHEN CONFRONTED WITH** a risky situation, a cat will delicately place little paws out as feelers. This first step is taken before committing to action. If the situation looks "doable", further exploration is warranted. If the initial foray proves to be too precarious, the cat will saunter off, looking as if it has something better to do and, in cool feline fashion, just take another course of action. Before rushing headlong into any exploit, take some time to figure out whether it's a trip you really want to take. If not, there's a good chance that you will find a more viable adventure around the corner. You could end up taking a new path, brimming with even greater possibilities than the first.

# *Graciously allow others to lend a hand*

✦ ✦ ✦

A CAT HAS difficulty reaching a few spots on its body and enjoys being stroked at these inaccessible places. By allowing others to lend a hand, you too can accept assistance in areas where you cannot readily help yourself. Let others rally round you and gain support during those times when you cannot easily do something on your own. It is not only in giving, but also in graciously receiving, that our lives are blessed.

# Have a well-groomed appearance

✦✧✦

**CLEAN IS THE** word. Cats, rightfully, enjoy a reputation for impeccable grooming. Much can be learned about keeping up appearances from the cat. They spend a third of their waking hours in self care. You can spruce yourself up and get ready to meet the world in much less time. By setting aside some unhurried moments for personal care each day, you show a regard for your body as a temple. By looking polished, you feel more confident as well as showing regard for the people you meet. If you have any house cats, just remember to brush their hairs off your clothing before you leave home!

# Have a treetop perspective

✻ ✻ ✻

SOME WILD CATS are arboreal by nature. Leopards sleep high in tree branches, using this elevation to their advantage. From the sheltered canopy of leaves, they can keep a lookout for their next meal or they can lounge, draped over a limb. You may also gain perspective by getting distance from your problems. From afar, everything appears smaller, including your worries. Imagine having the scope of the leopard's towering view, and then you too can search the landscape of your life for answers.

# Have good boundaries

✳ ✳ ✳

CATS ARE QUITE territorial and mark their terrain. In this way, they avoid border disputes. Clearly defined boundaries work well for humans too and make for good neighbors. Homes are a basic human necessity and the protection of them paramount. Staking out your domain mitigates the possibility of your place being disturbed. You can define not only your property boundaries but your personal boundaries, nicely but firmly. You can then, catlike, settle in and relax.

# Have two lairs

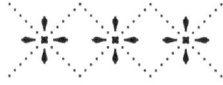

* * *

**TO PLAY IT** safe, the wild Jungle Cat frequently has more than one den in which it can retreat. You may want to consider doing the same. While the Jungle Cat's habitat may consist of thickets and reed beds, yours might consist of a comfortable sofa and a bed with a good mattress. Your home away from home doesn't need to be luxurious vacation quarters. It can be as simple as a *pied-a-terre* in town or a friend or relative's place to stay when the weather is bad or the weekly commute home is long. To have multiple lodgings is a good idea because, as this wild cat knows, it can be a jungle out there.

*Have you taken leave of your senses?*

✳✳✳

**WHEREAS CATS HAVE** a weaker sense of taste than humans, they make up for this by relying on a sharp sense of smell, keen sight, delicate sense of touch and incredible hearing. Humans often do not take into account the subtleties of their own five basic avenues of perception. You can begin to engage your senses more powerfully. Imagine getting caught in a rain shower while walking in a park, for example. Enjoy the cool wet spray touching your skin. Let your tongue catch and taste a few refreshing droplets of water. Watch the falling rain as it dances on the surface of a nearby frog pond. Listen to the drumming downpour against the paving stones. Smell the damp loamy soil mixed, perhaps, with the scent of nearby rose bushes. By soaking up the atmosphere, you are bound to be intoxicated by the *texture* of the world that surrounds you. Tag along with the cat. Come to your senses!

# Highlight your best feature

* * *

**CATS COME IN** a variety of colors. While few are solid in hue, the majority of cats have individual hairs that are differently colored at the tip than at the root. Some cats have shading that extends farther down the hair shaft. Some cats have darker hairs covering a pale undercoat, producing a smoky fur appearance. A cat may also have ticked fur, with alternating bands of light and dark coloration. The variation in tint contributes to the dramatic sheen and beauty of cat hair and contributes to a lovely coat. Likewise, you can highlight your hair color–and still not be afraid to show your roots! Want to amp up the fun? Try out some wigs. Now that's using your head!

# Investigate natural medicines

❉ ❉ ❉

MANY FELINES ARE not immune to the euphoric effects of catnip. Cats seen rolling around in what appears to be a state of bliss can attest to it. Think of it as their elaborate pantomime to demonstrate to you just how special an herb can be. As a member of the mint family, catnip is full of vitamins and has been used historically to treat a number of ailments, from the common cold to colic in babies, as it is known to have a sedative effect on humans. Cats serve as a reminder of the far-ranging, often medicinal, effects of herbal use. Take a tip from the cat. You too can explore the world of herbs and spices. Don't be surprised to learn that many of these botanicals may be of great benefit to you.

# *Keep waving*

❊ ❊ ❊

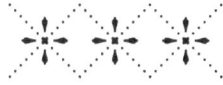

**LEGEND HAS IT** that the Greek historian, Herodotus, coined a name for the cat that means "tail-waver." Waving is a wonderful gesture. Royalty does it. Politicians do it. Sports champions do it. You can do it too. Give a wave and keep moving. When you haven't the leisure to chat, it's a great way of signaling friendliness to others without breaking your stride. The wave helps you to keep your free time to yourself instead of to your adoring public.

*Keep your ear
to the ground*

✢ ✤ ✢

**CATS LISTEN TO** the buzz. They are equipped with ears that can pivot faster than radar antenna to catch the latest murmurings and faintest whisperings. Once they receive intelligence regarding the source of the matter, cats act quickly. No anxious worry or debate. Try the cat's technique by tuning in to what's happening around you. Stay vigilant. Ask questions. By remaining alert, like the cat, you too can seize the day.

# *Know what you're protecting*

✳ ✳ ✳

TABBY CATS WITH certain coloration and markings can resemble a coiled snake when curled up, asleep. This snake camouflage evolved to help protect nocturnal felines while daylight napping in the great outdoors. This strategy of imitating a serpent does not stop with the fur ruse either. When feeling threatened, a cat will mimic the hissing and spitting of a venomous snake. Consider what you're defending next time you're having a hissy fit. It may be therapeutic.

# Know what you want and go after it

✠ ✠ ✠

**IF IT IS** neither fish nor fowl, cats aren't particularly interested–except in the case of rodents, where they play an exceptionally good game of cat and mouse. Simply put, cats know what is worth their while and what is not. They just aren't going to waste their precious time, period. You also needn't squander your days by putting your energy into useless pursuits. Next time that you are about to be sidetracked from your objective, remember the cat's single-mindedness of purpose. Find the most direct route to your goal and take it!

# *Land on your feet*

✳ ✳ ✳

**AS THE SAYING** goes, a cat has nine lives. The connection with nine may go back to the Egyptians, who, in their mythology, had The Ennead, meaning "the nine" deities. Twin lion gods, sister and brother Tefnut and Shu, were part of the nine. Sun god, Ra, the father of the other deities, was given a lion's head. In the middle ages, the cat was often perceived as a familiar of witches, leading to its persecution. However, the cat's frequent ability to literally land on its feet was taken to be lucky, and seemed to accord it nine lives. In a Christian context, it was a trinity of trinities, the mystical number nine. Take a cue from the cat. Trust that, whatever happens, you can handle it. Figuratively speaking, you too will be able to "land on your feet."

# Learn a new language – body language

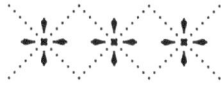

※ ※ ※

CATS KNOW THE universal, unspoken language of the body. It is the *lingua franca* of the animal kingdom. Cats may, for example, make themselves appear larger by turning sideways or arching their backs. They may "get their hackles up". In this way, cats can read one another and see where each other stands. The ability to send out and interpret body language is a good idea for people as well. This talent makes for a more socially skilled individual. When you learn to translate cues present in body language, studies show that you are receiving up to 93% of any communication message.

# Leave a legacy

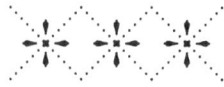

❖ ❖ ❖

ANCIENT EGYPTIANS REVERED the cat, and with good reason. Cats kept the mice population in check, ensuring that their stored crops were kept safe from the scourge of this rodent, a pest quite capable of eating the Egyptians out of house and home. Put simply, cats made themselves useful. They helped out while ever remaining true to their hunting nature. In medieval times, many families emblazoned their shields with the lion rampant as a symbol of valor, protection and defense. This historic emblem serves to encourage you to make your mark in life. By lending your unique talents, you will add your own legacy to the world.

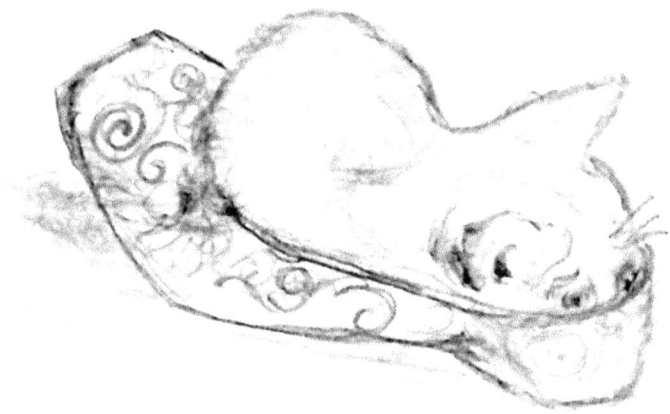

# *Live a charmed life*

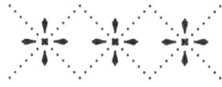

*❖ ❖ ❖*

IT HAS BEEN told that the prophet Mohammed, a great lover of cats, once cut off the sleeve of his garment rather than disturb a cat sleeping in his arm. Despite the ill treatment of cats in the middle ages, popes were known to love their personal cats. While it helps to be cute, more importantly, it pays to be charming. Down through the centuries, the ever-endearing and playful cat has spread happiness in its wake. As a result, the cat has, in the main, been greatly loved and esteemed throughout Europe, the Middle East and beyond. Think that those enchanting shoes are too big to fill? Throw yourself into them for a perfect fit. Be genuinely delightful and you're destined to nestle into a charmed life.

# Make a mansion out of a mole hill

✳ ✳ ✳

SMALLER THAN A house cat, the "ant-hill tiger" is an informal name given to the black-footed cat of Africa. As the smallest of the world's wild felines, it makes its den in abandoned termite hills or the burrowing networks of aardvarks or springhaas. No need to magnify your problem when a simple solution is at hand. "Don't make a mountain out of a mole hill." The little black-footed cat makes a home out of a termite hill. Out of a mole hill, you can make a mansion! Can you dig it?

# Make like the sphinx

❈ ❈ ❈

**THE ENIGMATIC LOOK** that cats sometimes convey can be disconcerting to the observer. The look has puzzled people for centuries. Consider that most imponderable of all felines, the monolithic limestone statue of the Sphinx just outside of Cairo. Scientists are still trying to figure out that Egyptian cat. You can adopt the inscrutable look that is a hallmark of the cat. Next time you are at the gaming table or involved in a negotiation, just remember to adopt your best poker face. Keep 'em guessing.

# Make room for possibilities

✳ ✳ ✳

IN ACCOMMODATING THE changing needs of her kittens, a mother will move them various times in the course of their upbringing. When they are first born, kittens need to be protected and kept sheltered from predators. As they grow and develop, they require more room to spar with each other, to roam about and to learn essential hunting skills. There are times in life when you may want to move or expand. It can be anything from the size of your desk or the dimensions of your home to the location of your dreams.

# *Meditate on repose*

❋ ❋ ❋

CATS CAN SIT in a meditative pose, gazing off into the distance, often for long periods of time. Afterwards, they look relaxed and ready to explore their world. You may find daily meditative sessions to be restorative and serve as a wonderful way to settle the mind, regroup and regain a sense of equilibrium.

# *Model the cat's courageous kin*

✣✣✣

MONGOOSES, ALONG WITH hyenas and civets, are fellow members of the Feliformia branch of the Order Carnivora. Like cats, they are agile creatures. If need be, a cat will stand up against an aggressor. Their not too distant cousin, the mongoose, is courageous too, particularly when wrestling with a cobra. While mongooses are quick and lithe and seemingly gentle, they stand up to these snakes and generally slay the slithering reptiles. Mongooses do not have immunity to viper venom but they know their strength when it comes to the cobra. Even if bitten by this snake, it would take several times the lethal dose of similarly sized animals to kill a mongoose. Knowing your own internal strength can give you the courage to fight for what is important to you. Take heart in the cat's brave little relative, the mongoose.

# Model the cat's family connections

✳ ✳ ✳

**ALTHOUGH SIMILAR IN** appearance and behavior to dogs, spotted hyenas are in fact related to cats and are in the Suborder Feliformia. Cats could do worse.

Contrary to the widespread belief that they only scavenge, spotted hyenas hunt nearly all the food they eat. They appear to be able to plan ahead and will assemble a larger hunting party for zebras, say, than for smaller game. They cooperate when problem solving and will teach new skills to the inexperienced.

Team work has, through the ages, been the hallmark of civilized societies around the world. Sharing knowledge with the novice—taking time to show someone the ropes—is an excellent way for you to participate in the dignified tradition of cooperating. This selfless act of helping the inexperienced is a great example of what the psychologist Erik Erickson called generativity—an optimism and interest in guiding the next generation. It is a healthy stage for anyone who reaches a senior position in life, at any age!

# Organize from the start

✴ ✴ ✴

NEWBORN KITTENS QUICKLY begin to prefer one particular spot when nursing and will return there again and again. Kittens, their sense of sight not yet developed, can quickly figure out where to suckle by smell. Confusion would reign if the scent were to be removed. Their disorientation would lead to tussles among litter mates. It points out that a good routine, without disruption, is not only good for kittens but for people as well. Making a schedule helps you to get through any potential chaos in your life. Organization can nurse you back to clarity.

# *Pay attention*

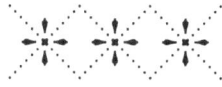

> ⁘ ⁘ ⁘

WASN'T THAT THE admonishment often made during school days? Cats seem to get on in the world by doing just that, paying attention. They are alert to even the subtlest shifts in their environment. Their observations turn to watchfulness as they gear up for action, if the situation necessitates. Attention requires practice. Take interest in your world and you will gain a lot from it. Life's a wonderful classroom in which you are always being tested on a variety of subjects to see how well you've mastered them. Cats know the score. You can join these sharp pupils who are successful in this field trip called life.

# Play against type

✳ ✳ ✳

**CATS ARE NOTORIOUS** for not liking water. Despite this general opinion, many cats enjoy, even thrive, in watery settings. Take the Fishing Cat, which has partly webbed feet. An ability to see underwater allows it to catch waterfowl from beneath the surface. Of the "roaring" cats, the leopard, the tiger and the jaguar excel in swimming. Other wild cats that are aquatically skilled include the Forest Cat, Ocelot, and the Flat Headed Cat, earlier known as the Fire Cat. Of the longhaired domestic breeds, the Turkish Van is so well suited to a wet environment that it lacks an undercoat, making for a quick dry after taking a dip. If you are the retiring sort, try a new sport. Do something unexpected. In short, be unpredictable.

# Play like a kitten to build a skill set

※ ※ ※

A KITTEN WILL naturally develop paw to eye coordination by playing with any small moving object that it finds. It will jump, spring, fling, flip, swing, pounce, snatch and bite into anything it fancies. In so doing, a kitten sharpens hunting techniques while imagining stalking and trapping. This play acting is suitable practice for gaining proficiency essential to both the quality and the length of its life. No wonder cats are such good hunters. At any age, you can learn a new set of skills while having fun doing it. Think of what you would like to become expert at, and then play with the idea of how best to pursue it!

# *Play the odds*

XXX

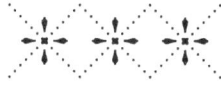

ALTHOUGH ONLY ONE in three attempts to catch a mouse is successful, the cat acts on odds that are still pretty good. The effort yields an excellent return. When making a decision, you too can benefit from determining the odds. Figuring out your probability of success ahead of time will help you to choose what you want to do and whether a course of action is worth the effort or the level of risk. After formulating your most favorable odds and after careful deliberation, trust your instincts. The cat does!

# Polish your dance technique

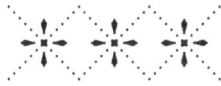

*✣ ✣ ✣*

REFERENCING THE RIGHTING reflex of a cat in free fall is the key to an important ballet technique. When tumbling from a height, the cat goes through a series of turning movements, rotating its head first and then twisting its body into alignment. A ballerina uses this technique on *terra firma*, when doing pirouettes. Called spotting, the dancer pivots her head around faster than the rest of her body. This method enables the performer to maintain balance while preventing dizziness. Prize fighters dancing around a boxing ring have been known to mimic the action of a cat in the hopes of copying the feline's lithe movements. Whether it's in a boxing ring, in a dance studio or on a ballroom floor, let the cat inspire you to put on your dancing shoes. Studies show that doing the tango or following the calls at a square dance improves brain functioning. Now that's a great way for dancers to step on something other than two left feet!

# Practice cat diplomacy

❊❊❊

FRIENDLY CAT BEHAVIOR includes greeting one another cheek to cheek, not unlike the old world custom of air kissing or giving a peck on each cheek. Cats may also engage in tail twining, similar to a warm hand shake in humans. Next time that you are at a social event, remember that an outgoing nature greases the wheels of a civilized world. Just consult the diplomatic corps in kittydom, and you will find that "pressing the flesh" is quite effective. Celebrate your common humanity with others by being an ambassador of goodwill.

# Practice on the job training

※ ※ ※

CATS LEARN ON the go. They "fake it until they make it" by pretending to know what's happening. Watch a cat who wants to follow you around. The cat tries to anticipate your move and runs well ahead of you, only to look back to get the gist of where you may be headed next. They could just as easily be asking as they glance back "Are you keeping up?" They quickly learn to look and act as if they are the leader. Try learning as you go. Sometimes real world experiences are the most direct route to learning how to do new things. Who knows, when you go casting about for ways to catch on, you just may land a "big one"

# *Prepare with a yawn*

✳ ✳ ✳

**CATS OFTEN YAWN** upon rising. Yawns stretch internal muscles and increase oxygenation. It is thought that people, like cats, yawn when they are feeling anxious. Perhaps all of these reasons account for the yawns that accompany many elite athletes before they compete in key events. These highly trained challengers need catlike alertness, precision and composure when they perform. Remember to yawn when you are feeling stressed, or at least take some deep breaths. Let those yawns be the calm before the storm of action.

# Pretend to be a secret agent

✳ ✳ ✳

**CATS MOVE QUIETLY** and with careful deliberation. You could say that they are the gumshoes of the animal kingdom. Cats, along with giraffes, camels, and sometimes elephants, are the only animals having a different gait from the rest of the quadrupeds. This manner of ambulating gives cats a quiet step and contributes to their superb ability to stalk prey. The cat's stealth provides them not only with a distinct advantage but also lends an aura of intrigue. With feline grace, you may just want to quietly show up somewhere, without fanfare. Surprise!

# Promote yourself

✳ ✳ ✳

**LEAVE THE PUBLICITY** to someone else and you may be waiting a long time. Why not toot your own horn? Lions roar not to scare prey, as they are ambush hunters, but to advertise themselves. This bellow is used by males to define turf, by females to announce her interest in mating, and by both to call for additional support and to communicate with one another. Self-promotion is sometimes necessary to get the job done. Speak up and let the world know that you are staking your claim!

_Pull yourself up by your_
_Puss'n Boots straps_

✤ ✤ ✤

**CATS ARE INDEPENDENT.** They usually hunt alone and rely on themselves. As a result they often appear to be capable and confident, and so they are. There comes a sense of pride in being able to do things yourself. You can become your "own person" with some perseverance and applied skill. While humans are necessarily interdependent creatures, there is still a time-honored place for whatever level of self-reliance you can muster. Be industrious and you are sure to find your way in the world.

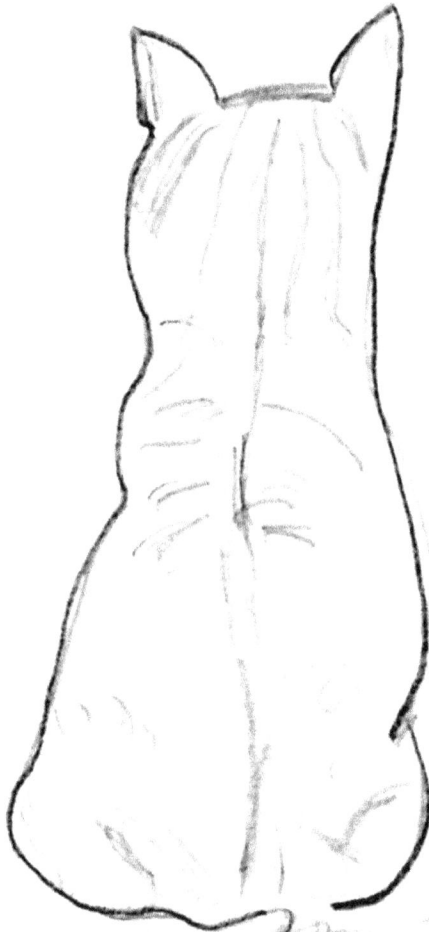

# *Reflect on catitudes*

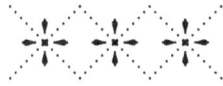

$$\text{:|: :|: :|:}$$

EVER EXPERIENCE A cat jumping up on a desk where you have been diligently working? With one tail sweep, it covers up or dispatches your paperwork to the floor. The cat's just doing a bit of needed house cleaning, that's all. Only a small matter of brushing the aggravating debris right out of its hair! When you take your work too seriously and the cat renders a contrary opinion, you can gain from adopting some feline *perspective*. Maybe you really ARE working too hard and attaching too much importance to the assignment. Take time out, even if you break only long enough to laugh at yourself.

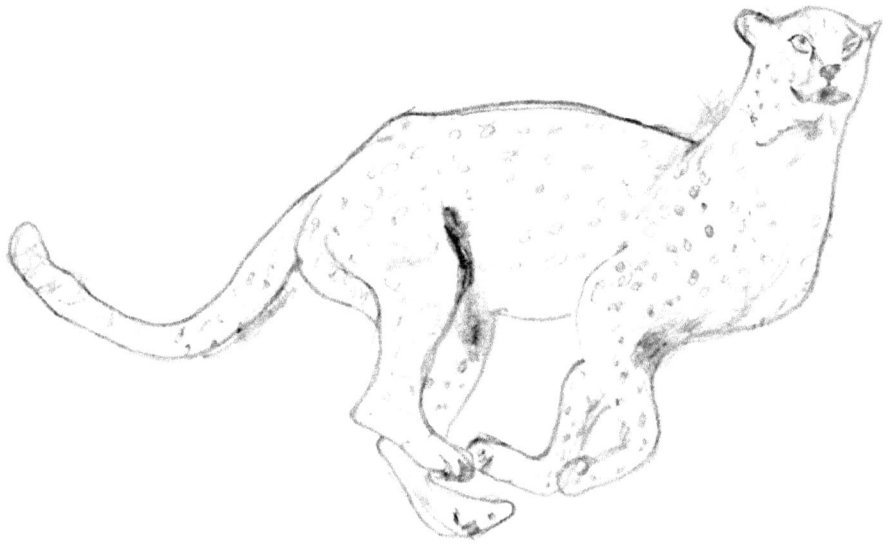

# *Remember that the race is to the swift*

✦ ✦ ✦

THE CHEETAH IS celebrated as the fastest land mammal on earth. As a member of the species A. jubatus, it is the only surviving member of the genus Acinonyx. Although the Cheetah is an unparalleled sprinter (it can accelerate from 0-60 in three seconds), it lacks staying power. There is a place for the marathon runner. There is also a place for the entrant in the 50 yard dash. You can be in the racing event of life by having a target goal and going the distance. If you find your stamina flagging and your fortitude being tested, you can win the race in many shorter energy spurts, just like the cheetah.

# *Revel in "alone time"*

THERE IS NO better model to show you how to appreciate being alone than the cat. Lounging, exploring, playing, the cat easily disengages from the dog-eat-dog world. As exemplar of independence, the cat knows how to enjoy its own company. Remember this, and you can relish those unfettered moments that you have when you are away from it all. This "down time" may serve to refresh you for the times when you are busily engaged with others.

# Run off and join the circus

‡ ‡ ‡

**THE BARBARY LION** once spanned the Atlas Mountains of North Africa. As the largest lion in the subspecies Panthera Leo Leo, they were the fiercest animals used in both the Circus Maximus and the Colosseum of ancient Rome. Thought to be extinct, the Barbary lion may have survived. Over the years, many big cats were acquired by zoos from traveling circuses. Today, a number of cats, believed to be Barbary Lions, can be found in several zoos as well as in park sanctuaries and game reserves. Ironically, despite the ongoing and legitimate debate over the use of animals in the circus arena, these magnificent beasts have been safeguarded from annihilation by the refuge that the circus provided. Whatever your version of the dream of "running off with the circus" may be, you might do well to follow that wish. Your life may depend on it!

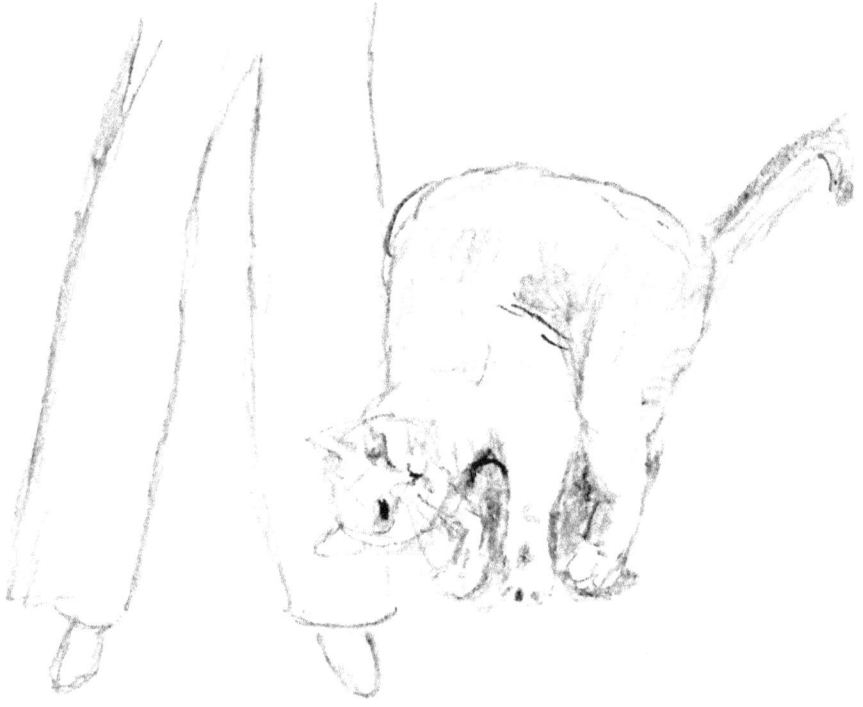

# Share your warmth

⁜ ⁜ ⁜

CATS WANTING TO get to know you better will make physical contact. They have glands on either side of their forehead that emit a scent that rubs off on you as they nuzzle against your leg. Using additional glands at the base of their tail, they sometimes encircle your legs, creating a pan-*aroma*. In the process of brushing against you, they also pick up your scent. Once they get your "essence", like a rare perfume, they will retreat and settle in. You too can savor the company you keep. Squeeze someone's hand or give a hug, sharing the joy of being alive.

# Sharpen your subtle wit

＊＊＊

WHILE CATS SPEND time sharpening their claws, these nails are usually kept well sheathed. They are drawn out when needed as a tool or a weapon, illustrating the old proverb "walk softly and carry a big stick." One can easily forget just how ferocious the adorable creature can be until it comes time to defend itself or its own. Unfortunately, people often mistake "might for right." The big bullies are feared while the unassuming are easily dismissed. You can be effective by being as reserved as the cat. Sharpen your verbal skills to parry those of your opponents but only skewer them with your sharpened and unsheathed wit as needed. *Touché!*

# *Stretch yourself*

※ ※ ※

WATCH A CAT in action and you will see that stretching is a routine activity. Often upon waking a cat will do some warm up moves before stirring about. Stretching does wonders. It helps with range of motion, reduces muscle tension, increases coordination, stimulates circulation and boosts energy. Yogis have captured the essence of these delightful stretches by employing them in a variety of feline yoga postures—the lion pose, the tiger pose, the sphinx pose and, of course, the cat pose. You too can make like a cat. Stretch and you will feel more alert so that you can begin to stretch your mind as well!

# Swing into Action

* * *

ALTHOUGH CATS MAY, at times, appear to be retiring, watch how they spring into action when fun and games are afoot. Racking up the balls may just be their cue to join in. When, at the billiard table in his Connecticut home, Mark Twain found his cats jumping onto the baize, he adjusted the rules of the game to incorporate their play.

Is there a game you'd like to try but stop yourself for fear of looking foolish? The cat is not inconvenienced by a little thing like the "how to" part of it. You needn't be either. Make up your own rules as you go along and see how quickly you learn to sink it in that corner pocket.

# *Take in the full dress production*

✳ ✳ ✳

CATS ARE GREAT observers. From them you can learn the great art of people watching. In a park, along a promenade, wherever you go, it's often amusing to view the antics of fellow humans. Take time to make an eyewitness account of your surroundings. Be in the audience of this open-air performance. It can be great theatre as well as an enlightening spectator sport!

# *Take side trips*

✻ ✻ ✻

CATS ARE GREAT at meandering around. They allow themselves the liberty of roaming about and seeing the sights, stopping to investigate anything that holds some interest for them. It could be a colony of ants crossing their path or the riveting appearance of a pigeon. A hidden garden may beckon them, a place where they'll encounter all sorts of flora and fauna. Follow the cat's lead. Allow yourself some unplanned and unstructured days where you can take off in a random direction, stopping by places that interest you and going where side trips beckon. The change of pace can be quite stimulating. Try it out. All sorts of adventures await you.

# Take things in stride

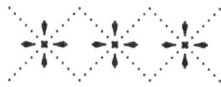

CATS UNDOUBTEDLY KNOW the score. As a result, they are often unperturbed by situations that would be disturbing to others. While they can be startled by sudden changes, cats readily adapt, taking an avid interest in what is happening around them. They have a remarkable ability to readjust and to know what to do. This *savoir faire* indicates that they are aware that the world isn't always about them and, as a result, have the poise to enjoy the pageant surrounding them. Knowing that on this grand-scale journey called life you share challenges with others on the path, you remember to take things in stride.

# *Try a little spontaneity*

**WHILE IT IS** generally prudent to exercise caution, cats do take chances in order to learn and to have fun. They are often on the lookout for enjoyable activities to engage in. Allow yourself to be more playful. Although swinging from the rafters may not be your idea of a good time, you can start by just being more spontaneous. You might surprise yourself and discover all sorts of astonishing delights along the way.

# *Value your distinctive features*

✦✦✦

DUE TO A mutation, the first cat of the Sphynx breed came into the world as a hairless kitten. Once reaching maturity, inbreeding was exploited to genetically reproduce this trait of hairlessness. It is a breed known to be sensitive and intelligent. This bald cat has the ability to alarm or attract, repel or fascinate, invite censure or praise. The Sphynx, in fact, does have hair but it is fine vellus hairs, similar to those found on human skin. The cat visually gives the shock of nakedness. Simultaneously, the Sphynx stuns with the beauty of its wedge shaped face and angular form. Regardless of your origin, your breeding, your appearance, whatever your genetic make-up, you are one of a kind. While critics may seem to be ever present, esteem not only yourself but your ideals and aspirations. You are a rare gem, of divine design.

# Vote with your feet

❉ ❉ ❉

THE CAT'S WALKIN' does the talkin'. If cats are bored, unin-terested or think that they have something better to do, they will get up and nonchalantly depart the scene. You too can vote with your feet. No need to be a prisoner of your own "shoulds". If you do not like a movie you've gone to see, for example, head for the nearest exit. Sometimes it's OK, even liberating, to just get up and leave. Follow that jaguar and cruise on out of there!

# "Waste not, want not"

✛ ✛ ✛

SOME CATS WILL save their leftovers for later. A dramatic example of this is seen in the leopard. As a great climber, the leopard can haul a carcass, one which is sometimes greater than its own weight, up a tree. This practice gives new meaning to the concept of "take out" food. The leopard might hunt and carry off a calf of the Kudu, for example, Wildebeest, or other antelope. If the leopard is not particularly interested in safeguarding the meat from marauders, it may actually leave the remains for scavengers. Either way, the meal is eaten. Since so much energy, time and sacrifice is required to meet the dietary needs of the leopard, the food is never wasted.

You can be a trustee of nature by not squandering its gifts. At home, save your leftovers and, when dining out, ask for a doggie bag.

# Wear loose clothing

✳ ✳ ✳

CATS HAVE LOOSE skin around their bodies. This extra "give" serves several functions. It makes life difficult for predators trying to get a hold on them. The extra skin provides cats with an excellent chance of slipping out of the maws of would-be assassins with their sights set on lunch. Loose skin also makes it easier for cats to move swiftly in a chase, without undue restriction. Additionally, they certainly look at ease in their skin. Wearing loose clothing that skims your body and putting on comfortable shoes gives you a similar freedom of movement, important when exercising and going about your busy day. Constricting fabric is not conducive to feeling at ease, not only during down time but also when you are active and needing to be at your best. Wear the proper attire and you can move more confidently and be your own style setter. As a bonus, you'll probably breathe a little easier.

# *Wind-up your dreams*

✳ ✳ ✳

**FORGET THE CHEETAH.** Even a domestic cat can out-run a human. Given the great disparity in size between cats and people, it is apparent that cats have superior sprinting gear. They remind us of a very important point. Cats have supreme confidence in their running skills because they've had loads of practice and because of their innate ability. They'll take off like a shot when they spot their chance to pursue their hunting goals. Likewise, you can "take off" in full confidence that your mind has the ability to both conceive of worthy goals as well as assist you in obtaining that which you desire. Run in the direction of your dreams. Like the cat, you already have the "right stuff" to realize your aspirations. Your desire and faith drives your dreams. Get going in pursuit of your objective. You will eventually wind-up at the goal post. The cat will be waiting for you there.

# Conclusion

✦ ✦ ✦

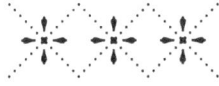

**FROM ONE OF** the tiniest of cats, a Blue Point Himalayan, weighing barely over a pound, to the Siberian tiger, that can weigh over 650 pounds, the magnificent cat truly does come in all shapes and sizes.

Be they adorable kittens or majestic lions, the felid family reveals a richly variegated group. Just look at your own clan to see the many differences in a shared gene pool. Look more broadly to all of humankind and see the great range of attributes to be found there. You may take heart in knowing that no one creature, be it a cat or a person, can do everything. Your worth derives from your own inner spirit. As this feline friend demonstrates—do your best, be your best and then release your cares. Adopt for yourself those traits that you most admire in the cat, be they the attributes of a courageous lion or its playful cub. Leaf through this book again and again and try out any "cat"egory that appeals to you. This simple style for living is a gift from the cats. The formula is spare and elegant. The best part is that their method can be adapted for humans. You too can take some tips from nature and learn to walk in the footsteps of some of the most beautiful life forms on earth--those charming members, and their relatives, of the Family Felidae.

www.ingramcontent.com/pod-product-compliance
Lightning Source LLC
LaVergne TN
LVHW011227080426
835509LV00005B/366